OCEAN

ATLANTIC
OCEAN

OCEAN

WHERE THE "WATER MONSTERS" LIVE
Habitats of the principal animals introduced in *Monster Myths*

PIRANHAS
South America: from Colombia to northern Argentina

ORCAS
Polar, temperate, and tropical waters worldwide

OCTOPUSES
Over 150 species in all the oceans
from the tropics to the Arctic and Antarctic

ALLIGATORS
7 species worldwide:
Southeast USA, Eastern China, Central and South America

CROCODILES
14 species worldwide:
Africa, Madagascar, Asia, East Indies, Australia, Central America,
Northern South America, West Indies, Southern Florida

GHARIALS
1 species worldwide:
Northern and Eastern India, Nepal, Pakistan, Bangladesh

SHARKS
GREAT WHITE SHARK
All tropical, subtropical, and temperate seas

BULL SHARK
North and South Pacific, North and South Atlantic, Indian oceans

TIGER SHARK
North and South Pacific (including coast of California, Canada and Alaska),
North and South Atlantic (including British Isles and Scandinavia),
Indian oceans

WHALE SHARK
Mid- and Southern Pacific
(including Australia), North and South Atlantic, Indian oceans

MONSTER MYTHS

MONSTER MYTHS

THE TRUTH ABOUT WATER MONSTERS

By Staton Rabin

A New England Aquarium Book

FRANKLIN WATTS
New York • London • Toronto • Sydney

ACKNOWLEDGMENTS

Special thanks to Sonny Allen and Mark Willett of Marine World Africa U.S.A. in Vallejo, California, and to Roddy Moscoso of the U.S. National Marine Fisheries Service.

**For Ruth Happel, Brandy, and my parents—
who know the whole story
—S. R.**

Frontispiece: According to legend, the arms of the kraken were so powerful that if they seized a ship's lines, the vessel was doomed to end up at the bottom of the sea.
Opposite half-title page: A deep-sea anglerfish.

Photographs copyright © : Norbert Wu: pp. 6, 12 bottom left, 22, 25 top, 26, 28, 30, 32, 43, 44, 45, 48, 49 bottom, 51; Fred Bavendam: pp. 7, 23, 24, 41 bottom, 47, 50, 52 bottom; Animals Animals: pp. 8, 16 (both Carl Roessler), 12 top, 20, 34 (all Zig Leszczynski), 12 bottom right (G.I. Bernard), 18 (Miriam Austerman), 25 bottom (Breck P. Kent), 29 (Richard Kolar), 33 (Tony Martin/OSF), 35 (Mickey Gibson), 36 (Ken Cole), 37 (Klaus Uhlenhut), 39 (Stouffer Productions Ltd.), 49 top (Scott Johnson); California Academy of Sciences/Caroline Kopp: p. 9; New England Aquarium/Paul Erickson: pp. 10, 11, 19, 52 top; Tom Campbell: pp. 13, 15; Loren McIntyre: p. 21; Jeff Rotman: p. 38; Andrew J. Martinez: p. 41 top; Sea Studios Inc.: p. 42; *National Geographic* Magazine, March, 1967: p. 46 (Robert F. Sisson).

The diagrams on page 10 are based on material from *Sharks: Silent Hunters of the Deep.* © Copyright 1986, Reader's Digest Press.

Library of Congress Cataloging-in-Publication Data

Rabin, Staton.
Monster myths : the truth about water monsters / by Staton Rabin.
p. cm.
"A New England Aquarium book."
Includes bibliographical references and index.
Summary: Provides information about the physical characteristics
and habits of such creatures as sharks, octopuses, alligators, and
barracuda as well as some of the myths about them.
ISBN 0-531-15222-7 (trade).—ISBN 0-531-11074-5 (lib. bdg.)
1. Aquatic animals—Juvenile literature. 2. Aquatic animals—
Folklore—Juvenile literature. 3. Sea monsters—Juvenile
literature. 4. Monsters—Juvenile literature. [1. Aquatic
animals. 2. Marine animals. 3. Sea monsters.] I. Title
II. Title: Water monsters.
QL120.R33   1992
591.92—dc20   91-34420 CIP AC

CONTENTS

INTRODUCTION 7

**CHAPTER ONE
SHARKS: DEMONS OF THE DEEP 9**

**CHAPTER TWO
PIRANHAS: CANNIBAL FISH 19**

**CHAPTER THREE
OCTOPUSES: EIGHT-ARMED BEASTS 23**

**CHAPTER FOUR
KILLER WHALES: WOLVES OF THE SEA 29**

**CHAPTER FIVE
ALLIGATORS AND CROCODILES:
THE MENACE WITH A GRIN 35**

**CHAPTER SIX
ROGUES' GALLERY:
AN UNDERWATER ROGUES' GALLERY 40**

HORSESHOE CRABS
JELLYFISHES
MORAY EELS
GIANT SQUID
BARRACUDA
STINGRAYS
GOOSEFISH
DEEP-SEA ANGLERFISHES
VENOMOUS AND POISONOUS ANIMALS

GLOSSARY 53

BIBLIOGRAPHY 54

INDEX 55

INTRODUCTION

Too often our earliest feelings about the animals that share space with us on planet Earth are based on fear, misunderstanding, and ignorance. Once established, these feelings are difficult to reverse—difficult, but not impossible.

The people who know the animal world best, the biologists and naturalists who spend countless hours observing animals in the field, use such words as "wonder," "fascination," and "respect" to describe creatures many of us find repulsive or frightening. This great difference in attitudes results, at least in part, from the scientists' greater knowledge.

The chances are that you don't have a very high opinion of some of the most celebrated animal "villains" of the world of water—sharks, piranhas, octopuses, killer whales, crocodiles and alligators, and others. If so, this book offers a good way to begin to change your mind. The purpose of *Monster Myths* is to allow you to take a closer look at those animals from the safety of your armchair; to give you a second chance to meet and appraise them. A deeper understanding of how and why those so-called villains live the way they do may help to replace your fear or revulsion with wonder, fascination, and respect.

But don't misunderstand the book's purpose. Given the right circumstances, it *is* reasonable to be cautious and even afraid of these animals. Some of them can be very dangerous indeed.

◄ A mass of menacing tentacles is what many people picture at the mention of an octopus. This reaction is very often based on a lack of understanding of the true nature of the water animal. ▼ A southern octopus jets through the water.

CHAPTER ONE
SHARKS
DEMONS OF THE DEEP

The scariest fish at San Francisco's Steinhart Aquarium doesn't swim, it doesn't eat, it doesn't breathe.

That's because the scariest fish at the Steinhart, a great white shark, isn't alive. It's frozen like a TV dinner at ten degrees below zero (minus 23.3 Celsius). Measuring over 13 feet (4 m) and weighing 1,500 pounds (680 kg), this toothy terror draws thousands of brave visitors to its refrigerator display case.

Why is it that even dead sharks frighten people more than most other animals do when they're alive? In part, the horror movies we see and books we read have convinced us that sharks *are* demons of the deep. And to us human beings, the sea is still a dark and mysterious place. In the sea the animals and the forces of nature—not humans—still reign supreme. Here the shark is king.

◄ The sight of a great white shark at close range is enough to inspire fear in even the largest and strongest of animals. There is no evidence, however, that great white sharks actively pursue human beings instead of their natural diet of seals, sea lions, and other animals of the sea. ▼ The great white shark at the Steinhart Aquarium.

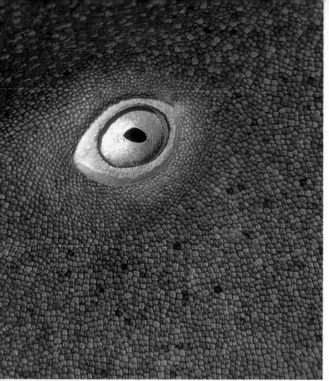

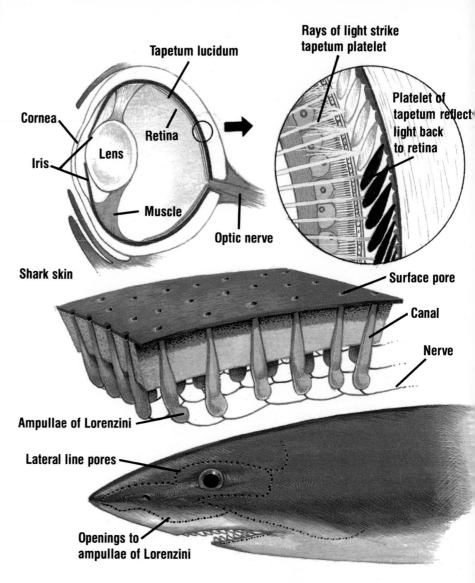

Rays of light strike tapetum platelet

Tapetum lucidum

Cornea

Iris

Lens

Retina

Muscle

Optic nerve

Platelet of tapetum reflect light back to retina

Shark skin

Surface pore

Canal

Nerve

Ampullae of Lorenzini

Lateral line pores

Openings to ampullae of Lorenzini

▲ Contrary to popular belief, sharks have good vision and can see shapes and even colors in their underwater world. Shark eyes, such as this nurse shark eye (above) have special reflecting structures at the back that help the shark see in the dim light of dusk, a favorite time to hunt for food. ▶ The shark's eye (top), the ampullae of Lorenzini (center), and the lateral line system.

It's been said that the shark is the perfectly designed killing machine. Like people, sharks are endowed with five senses—vision, touch, taste, smell, and hearing. They also enjoy two senses which people don't have: sensitivity to low-frequency vibrations in the water through their lateral line system, and the ability to detect electromagnetic fields.

Sharks use all of these senses to find their prey. They have generally good vision, including the ability to see colors and distinguish shapes. Their pupils, like ours, open and close depending on the surrounding light. A mirrorlike reflecting layer of cells behind their retina, called a tapetum, doubles the amount of light the eye receives. This makes sharks especially good hunters in the dim glow of twilight, a favorite time for predators.

Nostrils on the underside of the shark's snout contain cells so sensitive to smell that lemon sharks, for example, are able to detect one part tuna juice to 25 million parts seawater. Bottom-feeding sharks, like the nurse and horn shark, have sensitive whiskers called barbels to touch and taste their way around.

Sharks have ears that use a system of fluid-filled canals and ear stones to pick up vibrations in the surrounding water. They use this hearing in coordination with another organ sensitive to vibrations—the lateral line.

The lateral line is a row of pores along a fish's sides from head to tail. Tiny hairs in the pores sense changes in water pressure caused by the movements of other fish or predators. Some fishes use the lateral line to hold their position in a school. Sharks use this sixth sense to locate a struggling fish or other potential meals.

But what distinguishes shark senses from those of other fishes is a network of jelly-filled tubes called the ampullae of Lorenzini. Located around its snout, the ampullae of Lorenzini enable a shark to detect weak electric fields. This is an incredibly useful hunting tool to the shark, since all living creatures send out electric signals, produced, for example, by the pulsing of their hearts. A shark's sensitivity to electric fields is so sharp that, without interfering signals, it could probably detect your heartbeat in the ocean from a mile (1.6 km) away.

▼ The whiskerlike appendages that hang from the nurse shark's snout are called barbels, organs that help the shark explore the bottom mud or sand for food.

As far as a shark is concerned, everywhere you look there are more teeth. ▲ A preserved, gaping jaw of daggerlike teeth shows how wide some sharks can open up to snare their prey. ▼ Losing teeth is no problem for sharks, since another tooth rotates up as a replacement soon afterward. ► Even the shark's skin is composed of tiny teeth called dermal denticles, which explains why some people use sharkskin as sandpaper.

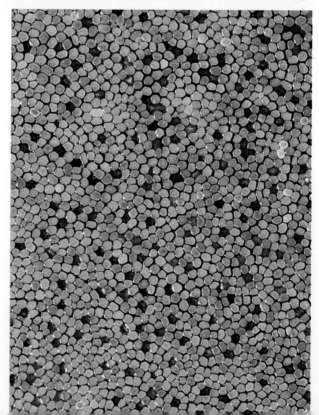

▲ Because its body is large and its uppermost fin is tall, the basking shark is often mistaken for a more dangerous kind of shark. Its mouth is gaping here to strain the water for its food—minute drifting animals called plankton.

Most sharks have powerful jaws. Depending on the species, a shark's jaw contains anywhere from six to twenty rows of teeth at all times. Although most shark teeth are sharp, they are constantly falling out. This is not a problem for the shark. As a tooth in the front row is lost or falls out, a replacement moves up escalator style. A young tiger shark, for example, can completely replace individual or even entire rows of teeth in a matter of a week. Sharks produce as many as 20,- to 30,000 teeth in a lifetime! Sharks even have teeth in their skin. Called denticles, these tiny projections make sharkskin as rough to the touch as sandpaper.

Ferocious sharks such as the great white shark and the tiger shark have been known to bite anything from tin cans to submarines. Great white sharks, or the "white death," as Australians call them, are especially fearsome creatures. Their huge, triangular teeth have serrated edges that can cut and tear flesh like steak knives. And with their massive jaws, one tooth tip of a great white can exert a pressure of 42,674 pounds per square inch (29,4237.2 kPa). By comparison a human tooth can manage a mere 150 pounds (1,034.3 kPa) of pressure per inch (one four-thousandth as much). Baby great white sharks start using their teeth early, eating their brothers and sisters while still in their mother's womb. It's no wonder that most people are afraid of sharks!

Still, there is little reason to fear most of these fishes. Not every shark is a great white. Out of the 350 or so known species of sharks, more than 300 would hurt you only if they were attacked or threatened.

Although large sharks tend to be more dangerous to humans than small ones, several of the biggest species are harmless. Basking sharks, which may grow as large as 50 feet (15.3 m), and the bizarre species megamouth have tiny teeth. Instead of meat, they eat only plankton. And consider the whale shark, not only the world's largest shark but also the largest fish that has ever lived—it may grow to a length of 59 feet (18 m) and weigh 13 tons (13,208 kg). This monstrous fish poses no threat to people.

Only three kinds of sharks are responsible for nearly all of the fatal attacks upon people. These are the great white, the bull, and the tiger. Great whites are the biggest flesh-eating sharks—the record length is 19.5 feet (5.9 m), though they probably reach 20 feet (6.1 m), and over 7,000 pounds (3,175.2 kg). Great whites are found in all oceans. But some scientists believe the bull shark may be even more dangerous than the great white because it is found not only in salt water but also in fresh and brackish water.

Some scientists believe that to a shark, you're about as delicious to eat as an old rubber tire. They base that belief on the fact that on the rare occasions when a shark attacks a human, it often takes one bite, spits out the flesh, then beats a hasty retreat. Those scientists say this means that sharks simply don't like the way people taste. Others believe this is simply the shark's normal method of attack. When a shark attacks a sea lion, it often takes a bite, then backs off to avoid being counterattacked. When its prey has bled to death, the shark returns to finish its meal.

Why do some sharks attack people? Scientists can only guess. Perhaps it's just a case of mistaken identity, a human taken for a seal, for example. On the other hand, it may be fear, not hunger, that causes such attacks. Sharks may feel threatened when a human enters their territory.

▲ Sharks, such as the gray reef shark of the Pacific Ocean, telegraph their readiness to attack by arching their body into a kind of S-curve. By understanding a shark's body language, divers can tell when a shark is threatening to attack and how close to approach before they place themselves in danger. The photo here of a Caribbean reef shark illustrates the kind of body flexing that indicates uneasiness.

Worldwide only about thirty people are killed by sharks each year. Overall, you are far more likely to die from a bee sting than be eaten by a shark.

If you need reasons to wish sharks no harm, there are many. They are an important source of protein for many of the world's peoples. Sharks also help prevent seals and sea lions from overpopulating their feeding grounds. Sharks may even provide us with medicines. For instance, scientists are researching a substance in shark cartilage which may be helpful in the fight against cancer. And shark corneas have been used to replace human ones, to allow the blind to see again.

Sharks are graceful and fascinating creatures. To know them may not be to love them. But now that you *understand* them, you may come to respect rather than fear them. And if more people in the world felt that way, we'd allow them to live in peace and go about their business, as they have for nearly 400 million years.

How can you be sure you'll never be eaten by a shark? These are some precautions recommended by marine biologists.

- Don't go swimming where the sharks are. If there's recently been a shark attack in the area, stay out of the water.
- Don't swim or dive alone—a friend might be able to help in an emergency.
- Don't swim when you have a cut or open wound, no matter how small. Although experiments cast some doubt that sharks have special interest in mammal blood (as opposed to fish blood, to which they *are* attracted), human blood may attract sharks.
- If you're spearfishing, don't stay in the water with dead or wounded fish.
- Don't swim near seals or sea lions, or stray too far offshore.
- If you use a surfboard, use a long board rather than a small body board. A person whose arms and legs are dangling from a little surfboard looks a lot like a shark's favorite food: a seal or sea lion.
- If you do see a shark, watch its body movements. Gray reef sharks, for example, signal their readiness to attack with an arching, back-twisting posture. If you see this body language, be alert for a possible attack.

And what do you do in the unlikely event that you encounter a real, live shark? Unfortunately, there is no such thing as a fully effective shark repellent. If you see a shark, don't panic. The more you splash and make a fuss, the more interesting you'll look to the shark. Instead, swim away quickly and get out of the water as soon as possible. If you're wearing scuba diving equipment, swim along the bottom to escape. There may be rocks and coral there to use as cover.

Meeting a shark doesn't necessarily mean it will attack you. It may just prefer to swim away. If it seems the shark is going to attack, use whatever weapons you have as a last resort. Otherwise, it's not a good idea to hurt the shark.

◀ In their quest to photograph a great white shark feeding, two underwater divers lure it into close range by dangling a piece of meat. The cage is there to make certain the great white doesn't include the divers as part of its next meal.

CHAPTER TWO

PIRANHAS

A hunter begins to lead his brave band across the dangerous Amazon River. Suddenly the water boils with movement. The man cries out, then vanishes. Five minutes later, a human skeleton floats to the surface of the river, the bones picked clean. The remaining hunters conclude that the man must have been eaten by piranhas.

Do stories like this really happen? Do piranhas really grab people and eat them?

Not really. Yes, piranhas have been known to attack people. But there's no evidence that people have been killed by them.

Piranhas are a type of fish that live in South American rivers and lakes. They range in size from a few inches to about 2 feet (.6 m). They have sharp teeth and powerful jaws, features which led the Tupi Indians to call them

◄ A head-on view of a red-bellied piranha, one of the more dangerous species, shows where it got its reputation. It can use its daggerlike teeth to tear pieces of flesh from its chosen prey, which doesn't include human beings. ▼ While the teeth of a meat-eating piranha's lower jaw are pointed and sharp, other kinds of piranhas have blunt and flattened teeth to crush seeds and fruits that fall from riverbank trees.

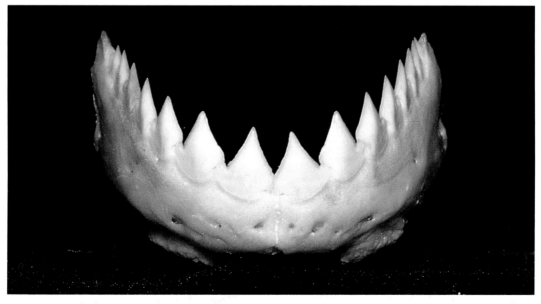

▲ Considering the piranha's fierce reputation, it is difficult to imagine it belongs to the same family of fishes as the colorful neon tetras shown swimming in a home aquarium.

pirai (fish) and *ranha* (tooth). One variety, the black piranha, could chew through a man's wrist in a couple of bites.

There are at least twenty species of piranhas, and most are completely harmless. Many are vegetarians which eat fruits and seeds that fall into the flooded river. So how do scary stories like our hunter episode get started?

Former United States President Teddy Roosevelt may be partly to blame. In his book *Through the Brazilian Wilderness* (1914), describing his trip to South America, he told hair-raising tales of "the most ferocious fish in the world . . . the piranha or cannibal fish . . . that eats men when it can get the chance." Blood in the water, said Roosevelt, "excites them to madness." Roosevelt's book was the first to give the average American notions about piranhas. Others soon followed. Even a respected Stanford University professor called piranhas "raging demons" that attack like lightning, clipping off fingers and toes "with the dispatch of a meat cleaver."

Care to take a swim with piranhas? South American children do; they know that piranhas are rarely dangerous to people. They know the conditions that make piranhas dangerous: usually only during times when the water level is low, thus limiting their food supply; or when it is breeding time and the males are naturally aggressive, do these fish pose a real threat. Then, they're likely to attack any animal that enters their territory. Piranhas also go after wounded prey, which includes humans. It may not be blood, but the movement of an animal in distress, that attracts them. And it is true that a school of piranhas can devour the flesh of a dead animal in minutes.

It's been said that piranhas can skeletonize a dead monkey in five minutes. Sometimes human corpses—victims of river accidents, for example—have been eaten by piranhas. But living human beings? Not likely.

So much attention is given to what piranhas eat that few people realize they are a delicious meal themselves, with a flavor akin to broiled bass or trout. Paraguay Indians sizzle piranhas on spits with other edible river fish. Besides enjoying piranhas' tasty flesh, natives of the Amazon Basin strip them of their jaws to use as an all-purpose cutting and sharpening tool.

Would you keep cousins of the piranha in your fish tank? Doesn't sound like a great idea. But common harmless neon tetras belong to the same family of fishes as piranhas, the family known as the *Characidae*. So do silver dollars, fish which get their name from their shiny silver appearance. So if you've ever had these fishes at home, you've owned relatives of piranhas.

Some people actually keep piranhas in their aquariums as pets. In some states, it's illegal to own piranhas. Occasionally, people tire of these pets and release them into rivers or lakes in the United States. Fortunately, most United States waters are too cold for piranhas to survive. Once in a blue moon, wildlife officials capture a piranha in U.S. waters. One was caught in Florida in 1970. But this is so rare, it really isn't anything to worry about.

So, the next time you come across those jungle adventure tales of people-gobbling piranhas, whether in a book, a movie, or on TV, don't believe everything you read or see.

▼ The piranhas pictured here are in a reversal of the roles people expect. Piranhas are usually a delicious meal for native diners rather than the other way around.

CHAPTER THREE

OCTOPUSES

EIGHT-ARMED BEASTS

The year was 1866, and Paris went "octopus crazy." There was octopus talk in all the cafes, octopus cuisine in the finest restaurants, octopus articles in French newspapers, even "octopus hats!"

What made octopuses the talk of the town was a novel by the French author Victor Hugo, *Toilers of the Sea*. In it the book's hero fights a deadly battle with the eight-armed beast in its undersea cave. Hugo called the octopus "supple as leather, tough as steel, cold as night." The author's tale frightened and fascinated Frenchmen. Soon after its publication, Hugo's wife wrote from Paris, "Everything here has become octopusied."

◄ The octopus can use a built-in siphon to expel water and propel its body gracefully through the ocean.   ▼ The stunning colors and patterns of the blue-ringed octopus make one forget it can deliver a dangerous and venomous bite to a careless underwater diver.

Are octopuses really the devil fish that fiction paints them to be? Are they really capable of wrestling human beings down to the seafloor?

There's no doubt that larger octopuses—and some grow up to 32 feet (9.8 m) across—are strong. One octopus kept in a public aquarium in Brighton, England, was able to pull the metal drain valve out of its tank. It's been estimated that if a 5-foot (1.5 m) octopus were holding on to something with all eight of its arms, it would take a quarter of a ton (226.8 kg) of force to pull the object free.

The secret of the octopus's strength is the suckers on its arms. These suckers act like the rubber suction cups on the ends of toy darts. Have you ever tried to pull a rubber dart from a target? Sometimes it can take all your strength to pull the dart free. But imagine if that dart were held to its target with the force of 1,920 suction cups! That's how many suckers—240 per arm—a common octopus has.

▼ The common reef octopus of the British West Indies prefers the cover of darkness for its excursions for the crabs and other marine invertebrates that make up its diet.

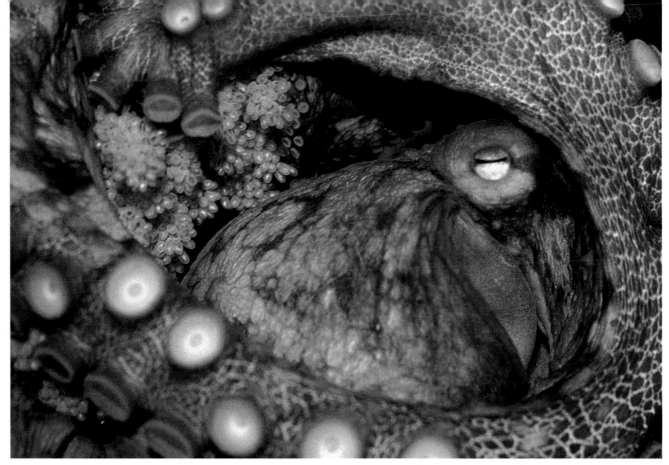

▲ An octopus's arms contain many disklike suckers that help it hold onto rocks or reef and to seize its prey. Here, a parent octopus cradles a patch of eggs and developing young.   ▼ Contrary to its reputation, the octopus prefers crabs to human beings.

Still, octopuses are hardly ever a threat to people. They're shy and timid invertebrates who hide in undersea caves or burrows in the sand or mud, and do most of their exploring at night. If one happens to grab you by the ankle or wrist with a rubbery arm, it will probably realize it has made a mistake and swim away. If not, you'll probably be able to free yourself quite easily. Octopuses' arms can't crush you the way boa constrictors' coils can.

There are two situations in which octopuses could be dangerous to humans: being bitten by one, and straying into a larger octopus's lair or territory.

Many octopuses have venomous bites. The tiny blue-ringed octopus, which is only about 6 inches (15.3 cm) across, has a particularly potent venom. This octopus is found in Australian waters. Left untreated, its bite could kill a person within a couple of hours.

A less likely scenario might occur if you happen to stray into a larger octopus's undersea lair, invade its territory, or try to handle or harass it. The octopus, feeling threatened, could then grab hold of you with its arms and might hold you underwater long enough for you to drown. But this scenario is unlikely to happen in real life.

In real life, octopuses are more concerned about getting caught than about catching you. They are food for moray eels, whales, seals, humans—and even other octopuses.

Octopuses have special methods of eluding predators. Over short distances, they can escape by sending out forceful jets of water which make for a high-speed getaway. Octopuses can also eject black or purple ink, clouding the water while they escape. Some scientists think the octopus ink temporarily confuses the sense of smell of the animal pursuing the octopus. This allows the octopus time to escape. It's also possible that the ink cloud's shape resembles the octopus itself, acting as a kind of decoy.

Octopuses deserve our wonder, not our fear. Any animal that can unscrew the top of a glass jar to get at the crab inside—something an octopus has been known to do—is capable of learning and solving simple problems. The well-developed brain and nervous system of octopuses have helped us better understand how our own bodies work. And experiments have shown octopuses' eyes (as well as the eyes of other cephalopods such as the squid) to be more closely matched with our eyes and other vertebrates' eyes, than are those of any other group of invertebrates.

◄ If all other defenses fail, an octopus can confuse a predator by releasing an inky fluid from a special ink sac.

CHAPTER FOUR

KILLER WHALES

WOLVES OF THE SEA

The Germans once called them *mordwal*—murder whales. Others call them orcas, wolves of the sea, or just plain killer whales. Nearly everyone agrees that these mammals are among the most ferocious predators in the ocean. So can they possibly be the same lovable creatures who give you a big, sloppy wet kiss at Sea World?

The answer to that question is a resounding yes. But until about twenty-five years ago, most people knew only that killer whales were ferocious predators. Today we also know about the lovable side of their nature. Long ago, Spanish whalers named them whale killers because they hunted other species of whales. Sometimes orcas would help whalers capture bigger

◄ Adult male orcas can reach a length of 30 feet (9.4 m), and meeting one underwater can leave a lasting impression. Orcas are graceful, strong swimmers that seize and consume their prey with powerful, cone-shaped teeth. ▼ Orcas travel in social groups called pods and cooperate in hunting their natural diet of other whales, sharks (even white sharks), fishes, seals, and sea lions.

Top of head focuses sound

Lower jaw

Returning echo

Transmitted sound

▲ How an orca is thought to echolocate. ◀ A pair of underwater scuba divers are dwarfed by a 45-foot (13.7-m) long whale shark. Despite its size, the whale shark's diet is made up of floating plankton, often smaller than the size of a matchstick.

whales. The whalers would reward the orcas with the dead whale's tongue, a favorite treat. Somehow "whale killers" got mistranslated to "killer whales," and a legend was born.

What is fact, not legend, is that killer whales are clever and powerful hunters. An adult male can grow up to 31 feet (9.4 m) long and weigh 9 tons (9,144 kg). If you combine this formidable size with a formidable set of teeth and an equally formidable brain, you can see why killer whales are such successful predators.

Killer whales travel in family groups called pods. A pod is made up of four to forty whales. When hunting, the members of a pod cooperate to capture and kill prey. Like wolves, they hunt in packs.

In a process called echolocation or sonar, the whales emit sounds which echo back to help them locate the fish, seal, or other animal they seek. Some scientists believe killer whales may also use sonar to stun fish before eating them.

Here's how a pod might go about capturing a seal. The seal is snoozing on an ice floe. The pod is swimming nearby. The whales pop their heads out of the water to have a look around. They see the seal and plan their attack. Quickly the whales swim toward the ice floe, cooperating to stir up a

▲ The whale shark is the largest living fish on Earth. It uses specially adapted gill arches to act as a sieve and collect its primary diet of small plankton.

giant wave. The wave washes over the seal, knocking it into the water, and that's the end of the seal. A killer whale can cut a seal in half with a single bite.

An average adult male orca can eat as much as 550 pounds (249.5 kg) of food per day. So these whales must spend a lot of their time hunting. Some pods specialize in feeding on marine mammals; others eat mostly fish. But there's no evidence that killer whales go looking for human beings to eat.

Killer whales live in every ocean of the world, though mostly in colder waters. Except for humans, no other creature represents a threat to them, not even sharks.

From the days of Basque whaling in the twelfth century right up to the present day, whales have been relentlessly hunted for their meat, their oil, and other commercial products derived from them. Fortunately, whaling is now banned nearly everywhere in the world. As of 1986 the member nations of the International Whaling Commission have stopped their commercial whaling. However, the worldwide ban on hunting whales doesn't pertain to certain groups who need them for survival—Eskimos, for example—or to whaling for research. Still, while not now in danger of extinction, killer whales are threatened. Loss of habitat and environmental pollution are the greatest of these threats.

Despite the threat of human abuse, killer whales genuinely seem to like people. If the name "killer whale" still sounds scary to you, you could think of this mammal as a very big dolphin. If you love dolphins, maybe you can learn to love killer whales.

▼ This view of the butchering of a finback whale at a whaling station in Iceland is a scene from the past. Thanks to the Marine Mammal Protection Act of 1972 and a 1986 moratorium by member nations of the International Whaling Commission, whaling has come to a standstill.

CHAPTER FIVE

ALLIGATORS
AND
CROCODILES

THE MENACE WITH A GRIN

How cheerfully he seems to grin
How neatly spreads his claws
And welcomes little fishes in,
With gently smiling jaws.

—Lewis Carroll
Alice's Adventures in Wonderland

The crocodile in James M. Barrie's popular tale *Peter Pan* has swallowed a ticking clock. Whenever Captain Hook hears that ticking, he knows the bloodthirsty crocodile that wants to eat him is headed his way and he's able to escape. But, what happens when the clock winds down? Then the crocodile can quietly sneak up on Hook and finish him off!

◄ Contrary to their bloodthirsty image, this scene of alligators feeding is an unusual sight. As with other monsters of myth, these animals deserve our curiosity and respect, and awareness of when they are potentially dangerous and when they are not. ▼ One reason the saltwater crocodile is an endangered crocodilian is that it doesn't begin breeding until the comparatively late age of ten. In addition, hunters and the destruction of its habitat don't allow it much chance to reproduce its kind.

▲ The American alligator (shown here) and the Chinese alligator can tolerate lower temperatures than most of their relatives which are limited to the tropics. Government protection has helped the American alligator recover; its Chinese cousin, however, remains endangered.

Actually, there's a grain of truth in the way Barrie depicts the crocodile. No, crocodiles don't really swallow clocks. But it's true that crocodiles are very sneaky when stalking their prey. They drift along in the water, with only their nose and eyes showing above the surface. Silently they watch and wait for their victims. Sometimes, crocodiles will hang around water holes, where they know other animals come to drink.

You may be wondering what the difference is between an alligator and a crocodile. Crocodiles tend to be bigger and more aggressive than alligators. Crocodiles usually have pointed snouts, and alligators blunt ones. When a crocodile's mouth is closed, the fourth tooth on its lower jaw protrudes, giving the appearance of a toothy grin. Alligators look a bit less like they need a good orthodontist. Their fourth tooth fits into a special slot on the upper jaw and isn't visible.

Of course, alligators and crocodiles don't ever choose a particular person (like poor Captain Hook) as their favorite victim. And most crocodilians—the group of reptiles that includes alligators, gharials, crocodiles, and their South American cousins, the caimans—never eat people. Only two species of crocodilians have claimed a fairly large number of human victims over the years: the Nile crocodile, the one you see Tarzan wrestling with in those old Hollywood movies, and the Indo-Pacific crocodile, Australian actor Paul Hogan's costar in *Crocodile Dundee*. Both of these reptiles can grow to 20 feet (6.1 m) or more. That's the main reason why they're dangerous to people. Only Tarzan can win a wrestling match with one of these big crocs. Their usual prey are mammals, birds, fish, and other reptiles. A large Nile crocodile will even eat zebras, warthogs, cattle, and antelope. And if a careless person happens to swim in its territory, he or she may just be one more good meal to the crocodile. It isn't picky.

Millions of people in Africa, Asia, and Australia interact with crocodilians every day. Very few of them are attacked, much less eaten. People wash their clothes in African lakes and rivers, swim, and go boating, and most of the time nothing bad happens to them.

▼ Although the saltwater crocodile has been known to kill human beings, its normal diet consists of birds, as shown here, and small mammals, fish, and shellfish. Crocodilians sneak up on a bird and pull it underwater.

Are there any crocodilians in the United States? If you live in Florida, you may know the answer. Although they were once a threatened species, there are American alligators in Florida and other parts of the southeastern United States. Texas, too, has alligators. The United States now has strict laws protecting them because they were nearly hunted to extinction for their skins, which people used to make alligator purses, belts, and luggage. Baby alligators were even stuffed as toys. In 1888, just ten hunters in Florida killed 5,000 alligators. And in 1907 a single company in Louisiana made leather out of 500,000 crocodile skins. By the 1960s the American alligator was in real danger of disappearing. Today, in the United States and in many other countries of the world, the hunting and export/import of crocodilian skins is limited by law. But people often ignore these laws because crocodilian skins are big business.

Some crocodilian species are endangered, but in the United States the once threatened American alligator is slowly making a comeback.

Crocodilians today appear much as their relatives did back in the Age of Reptiles, when huge dinosaurs roamed the Earth. Like the shark, crocodilians have survived millions of years of evolution largely unchanged. In a way, they are our window on an era long disappeared. They are survivors well-suited to the environment where they live. This ability to survive for such a long time deserves far more attention than their supposedly menacing grin.

▼ Crocodiles will survive in the wild only if crocodile hunters such as these people from the region of Lake Turkana in Kenya, Africa, limit the number of animals they take to what their families need. The reason many of these animals are threatened with extinction is overhunting and destruction of their natural habitat.

HOW TO RESPECT A CROCODILE

How do you avoid getting eaten by a crocodile? Read the signs. Most places that have crocodiles as frequent visitors have signs warning you of their presence. Take the signs seriously. Even if you don't see any crocodiles, they may still be there.

Crocodilians rarely attack on land. Still, if you're fishing on a riverbank, stand back at least 10 feet (3.1 m) from the edge. At night (when crocodiles do most of their hunting) stand back even farther. A slow-moving crocodile can make a surprisingly swift grab at the water's edge if your foot is within its reach.

▼ The main difference between an alligator and the American crocodile, shown here, lies in a large fourth tooth on the lower jaw. In the alligator and caiman, this tooth disappears into a pit in the upper jaw when the mouth is closed. In crocodiles, the tooth remains visible.

CHAPTER SIX

ROGUES' GALLERY

AN UNDERWATER ROGUES' GALLERY

So far in this book you've encountered sharks, piranhas, octopuses, killer whales, and alligators and crocodiles. But what about other water animals with villainous reputations? The following rogues' gallery showcases animals that are alive and well in today's oceans and seas, unlike such mythical animals as the Loch Ness Monster or the dinosaurlike Mikele Mbembe of Central Africa. This list will undoubtedly continue to grow as we explore the depths of the ocean to discover animals we have never seen before. The 15-foot-long (4.6-m) deepwater megamouth is a good example of such a discovery.

The best questions to ask if you encounter an animal you've never seen before are:

1. Is it territorial? Will it attack others who approach its territory?
2. If it attacks, does it cause harm?
3. Will it eat you? Are you food?
4. Could it mistake you for a potential mate?
5. Will it perceive you as dangerous if you advance or move on it?

With these questions in mind, let's meet nine more water monsters.

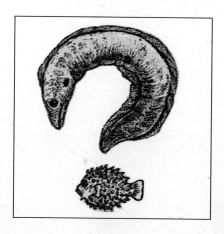

HORSESHOE CRABS

DESCRIPTION AND SIZE There are four species of horseshoe crabs worldwide, and they live along the Atlantic coast of North America and the Southeast coasts of Asia. Named because of their shells' horseshoe shapes, these marine invertebrates can grow to an adult size of 23.6 inches (60 cm).

HABITS AND HABITAT Horseshoe crabs are scavengers of food such as clams and worms in shallow water on sandy or muddy shores.

MYTH The horseshoe crab's tail, spine, and underside appendages inflict painful and venomous wounds.

TRUTH BEHIND THE MYTH The feared appendages are the animal's pincers and walking legs, which are harmless. The tail is used to turn the animal over if it lands on its back. It may also help it burrow in the sand. The tail does not contain a venomous barb like that of stingrays.

SPECIAL FEATURES The blood of horseshoe crabs is an important tool to detect infection in humans. Substances in the blood can help doctors detect signs of diseases such as spinal meningitis. Research on the horseshoe crab's eye has helped scientists understand human vision and the way our nervous system works. Sometimes called living dinosaurs, horseshoe crabs have remained essentially unchanged for over 300 million years of evolution.

▲ ▼ The horseshoe crab's tail, walking legs, and mouth parts neither inflict painful wounds nor inject venom. They are simply means for the crab to right itself after it has been turned over, to move around, and to feed on its natural diet of shellfish and worms. The platelike structures near its tail contain gills.

JELLYFISHES

DESCRIPTION AND SIZE There are about 200 different kinds of jellyfishes worldwide. Jellyfishes are relatives of other stinging animals such as corals and sea anemones. The bell of the common white moon jelly (*Aurelia aurita*) of the North Atlantic and the Mediterranean grows to be 9.8 inches (25 cm) and more, while that of the lion's mane jellyfish (*Cyanea capillata*) can reach 3 feet (1 m) across.

HABITS AND HABITAT The jellyfishes we see near the surface of the water are in the swimming stage of this animal's life history. In the other stage they attach to some underwater surface by means of a stalk. Jellyfishes are solitary swimmers, and they are exclusively saltwater animals.

MYTHS All jellyfishes inflict severe and dangerous stings. The best way to get rid of them is to cut them into many pieces.

TRUTHS BEHIND THE MYTHS Jellyfishes' tentacles contain stinging cells called nematocysts, which they use to capture and paralyze plankton and small fishes, not scuba divers. While it is true that all jellyfishes have stinging cells, many species, such as the moon jelly, are too weak to penetrate human skin. The red or pink lion's mane jellyfish deserves caution as it can inflict a painful rash, especially if a swimmer encounters a group of them.

Another animal often called a jellyfish, the Portugese man-of-war is actually a siphonophore. It is not a true jellyfish because it consists of a colony of animals rather than an individual. The Portugese man-of-war can produce a powerful sting, but that sting usually is not fatal.

The most dangerous of all true jellyfishes are not the largest. They are small tropical animals called sea wasps or box jellies, and their venom can be fatal to humans.

And cutting jellyfishes into pieces not only is not the best way to get rid of them, but it also often results in each piece regenerating into new adults.

SPECIAL FEATURES Jellyfishes are animals of extraordinary beauty. They are relatives of the animal responsible for one of the most diverse and life-rich ecosystems on Earth—the coral polyp which builds the coral reef. The study of the jellyfishes' stinging cells has led to the development of useful medicines for humans.

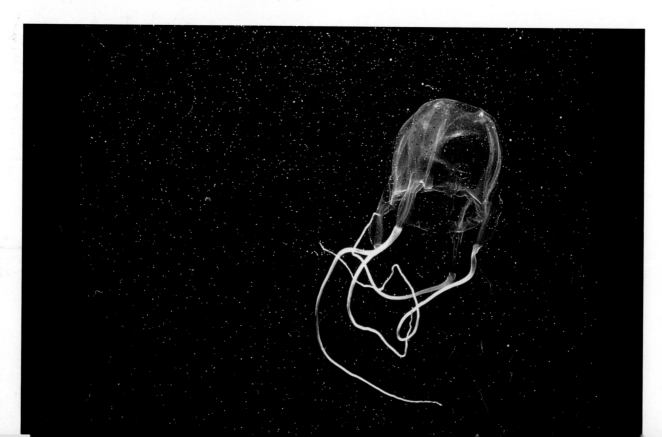

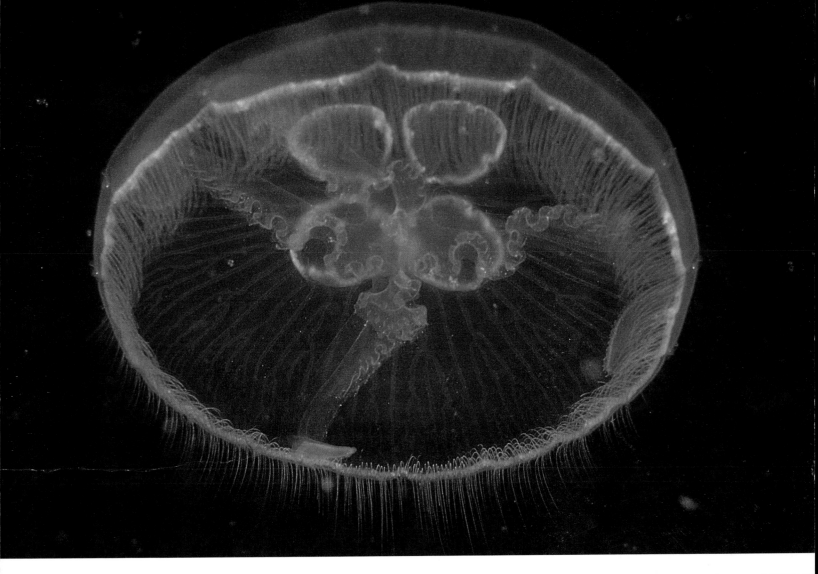

▲ Once a jellyfish or other jelly animal has gained a bad reputation, *all* jellyfishes become suspect. Although the moon or white jellyfish's short tentacles do have stinging cells, they are generally harmless to human touch. ◄ Other white jellyfish called sea wasps, on the other hand, can deliver a powerful, dangerous sting. ► The tentacles of the lion's mane jellyfish (right) contain stinging cells that paralyze its prey of fish and plankton, and can cause a painful rash on a swimmer.

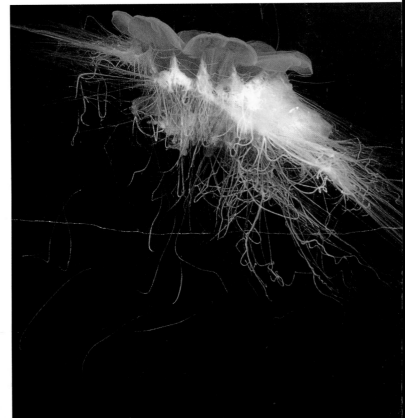

MORAY EELS

DESCRIPTION AND SIZE At least eight species exist worldwide, including the Mediterranean moray eel, which can grow over 6.5 feet (2 m) long. Most morays mature at 4 to 5 feet (1.2– 1.5 m).

HABITS AND HABITAT Moray eels are found in all tropical seas. Although they most often live in shallow waters, they occasionally enter fresh water. Moray eels are territorial and remain in caves or burrows during the day, emerging to feed on favorite foods such as octopus and lobster during the night.

MYTHS Moray eels are deliberately aggressive toward humans. Their bite is venomous and once a moray bites you, it doesn't let go.

TRUTHS BEHIND THE MYTHS Morays are generally shy and retiring animals which prefer to stay in the protection of a burrow, or cave. They are not aggressive toward human divers unless they are provoked or their territory is invaded or they mistake a finger for a piece of food. There *is* real danger if a diver provokes a moray, because the eel could respond by biting the person. Death could result if the diver is bitten in a vulnerable spot, such as an artery. However, if bitten in a less vulnerable part of the body, the most the diver has to fear is that an infection could be caused by the bacterial slime on the moray's teeth. But no human has ever been poisoned by "moray venom" because they have no venom to inject.

SPECIAL FEATURES Some morays have long, thin teeth to hold on to their prey while other species have blunt teeth to crush and eat crabs. Moray eels can be extraordinarily colorful; one species, *Rhinomuraena quaesita*, sports turquoise, bright yellow, white, and blue colors.

◄ The ribbon eel (a moray with the scientific name of *Rhinomuraena quaesita*), and ► the spotted or dragon moray are sometimes seen in public or home aquariums, where they are admired for their dazzling colors and patterns. ▼ The popular image of the moray eel is of a den of squirming creatures intent on attacking everything that moves. Moray eels are more likely to be found hiding in well-protected caves (below), waiting to hunt for food under cover of darkness.

GIANT SQUID

DESCRIPTION AND SIZE One giant squid, *Architeuthis*, which was washed up on Plum Island beach off the coast of Massachusetts in the 1980s, was estimated to measure 32.8 feet (10 m) from its head to the end of its longest tentacle. Giant squid are said to reach lengths of 60 feet (18.3 m) and weigh 1,000 pounds (450 kg) or more. Giant-squid eyes can measure up to 10 inches (25 cm) in diameter.

HABITS AND HABITAT Giant squid are found in oceans throughout the world, especially in deep water. They feed on a diet of fish, mollusks, and crustaceans. Like other squid, *Architeuthis* has eight thick arms and two longer tentacles to capture prey and bring it into its beaked and parrot-like mouth. Fins along its head propel the giant squid's movement, but the squid can also force water through a built-in funnel, enabling it to accelerate quickly. Giant squid release ink from a special ink sac as a defense, especially against its chief predator, the sperm whale.

MYTH Giant squid and giant octopuses ruthlessly attack everything from submarines and sailing ships to giant whales. Kraken, a legendary deep-sea monster of the Middle Ages, was said to have been a giant octopus or squid.

TRUTH BEHIND THE MYTH Although giant squid have the size and power to seize large objects, there is no evidence to support their alleged unprovoked attacks on large vessels.

SPECIAL FEATURES Thanks to their large, and therefore more easily studied, nerve fibers, including their eyes' optic nerves, squid are a good example of an animal that has helped scientists to better understand the workings of the human nervous system. They also have a huge potential as an animal for mariculture—growing fish on special ocean farms for later sale in restaurants and commercial markets. The people of the Orient and the Mediterranean have long considered squid a special delicacy.

▲ A young specimen of the giant squid *Architeuthis* was found in Trinity Bay, Newfoundland, in October 1965. It measured 21.5 feet (6.6 m) from the tip of its tentacle to the end of its mantle.

BARRACUDA

DESCRIPTION AND SIZE There are twenty species of barracuda, the largest of which are thought to be no longer than 6 feet (1.8 m). A slender torpedo shape and a lower jaw with razor-sharp teeth jutting ahead of the upper jaw give the barracuda a very recognizable profile.

HABITS AND HABITAT Barracuda are usually found in tropical salt waters, especially around coral reefs, but they may appear in cooler temperate seas as well.

MYTHS Barracuda are invariably aggressive predators which attack humans and fishes alike. Their flesh is poisonous and should never be eaten.

TRUTH BEHIND THE MYTHS Despite their impressive array of sharp teeth and their curiosity

▲ The few times that barracuda have become dangerous to human beings is when they mistake the glint of an underwater diver for natural prey such as a school of fish.

in approaching divers, barracuda seldom attack humans unless provoked, or unless they're in turbid (cloudy or muddy) waters where they might mistake the glint of a scuba tank for a fish. Their ability to inflict a nasty wound should not be overlooked, however, and they deserve respect.

SPECIAL FEATURES Barracuda are highly efficient and effective predators of other fishes. Extremely stealthy creatures, they hover in the water then lunge with lightning speed to attack their prey. Though their streamlined body allows them to achieve short bursts of tremendous swimming speed, they are unable to maintain that top speed for long periods of time.

STINGRAYS

DESCRIPTION AND SIZE Pancakelike in appearance, stingrays come from the family of skates and rays, which flap large winglike side fins (pectoral fins) to move around. There are about 100 different species of stingrays worldwide. Species range in size from the Atlantic stingray, about a foot (.3 m) in diameter, to the largest species, the Indo-Pacific smooth stingray, whose total length can be 15 feet (5 m) with a diameter of over 7 feet (2 m). Stingrays get their name from the one or more spines on the top side of their tail which contain venom sacs.

HABITS AND HABITAT Stingrays inhabit tropical and subtropical oceans, although some move into cooler waters in the summer; several species live in fresh water in South America, where they scavenge and hide in shallow, mud-bottomed rivers. Stingrays eat fish, mollusks, and crustaceans with their blunt crushing teeth.

MYTHS Stingrays are able to shoot with their spines and to deliver lethal injections of their venom.

TRUTHS BEHIND THE MYTHS Many people assume all rays have poison spines or emit electricity, not realizing that many, such as the immense manta ray—wingspan 20 feet (6 m)—have no such protection at all. With their mouths and gills on their underside, stingrays have a devilish appearance contradicted by their generally unaggressive behavior. The spines and venom sacs are used for defense, and although they can cause a painful wound, it is rarely fatal. The bigger species, such as the Indo-Pacific stingray, with a 1-foot-long (30 cm) spine, can inflict an especially dangerous wound.

And a stringray's spine must come in contact with its victim's skin to deliver an injection of venom. The animal is not able to shoot its venom.

SPECIAL FEATURES Many people who fish consider skates and rays delicious. They also play an important role as bottom scavengers, cleaning the bottom around bays and coastal shelves.

▼ Once the barb on a stingray's tail has penetrated its victim, its inward pointing design makes certain it won't be dislodged easily. Barefoot and careless waders are sometimes at the receiving end of a painful wound. ▶ Like the whale shark and basking shark, this giant of the ray family called a manta ray is a harmless filter feeder whose only threat to people is if it lands on someone after a powerful leap out of the water. ▶ Below left: A view of the mouth and underside of a giant stingray. Below right: Although this stingray's stinger is plainly visible here, it is much less obvious when it lies buried in the sand.

GOOSEFISH

DESCRIPTION AND SIZE Goosefish are part of a larger group of fishes known as anglerfishes, named for a specially modified spine near their mouth which they use to lure, then swallow, prey. There are about twelve species of goosefish worldwide. The largest goosefish grows to a length of over 4 feet (1.2 m). Its Cheshire-cat grin, immensely wide mouth, and menacing teeth give it a ghoulish, frightening appearance.

HABITS AND HABITAT Goosefish inhabit tropical and temperate marine waters everywhere except the eastern Pacific ocean. With their somewhat pancake-flat bodies, they hunt and rest lying on the ocean floor, often well camouflaged because of their color and fleshy fringes that match their surroundings. Goosefish have been known to consume everything from fishes and crabs to sharks and water birds.

MYTH Because of their repulsive appearance and huge appetite and size, goosefish are as aggressive toward people as they are toward their normal prey.

TRUTH BEHIND THE MYTH The appearance of an animal is not a reliable guide to its behavior toward humans. The frightening appearance of the goosefish serves a useful role as a disguise that helps it to hunt efficiently. Available evidence suggests that goosefish seldom attack people and that such attacks that occur usually result when the animals react defensively to a perceived threat.

SPECIAL FEATURES If you have ever eaten monkfish, which is available in restaurants and fish markets, then you have eaten a goosefish. Its meat, which is gaining popularity in the United States, is already considered a delicacy in Japan and northern Europe.

▶ Above: A goosefish eats anything from ducks to fishes to an old rubber boot. Human beings are not on their menu. ▶ Below: This cavernous mouth looks like danger to the unwary diver. But the goosefish gets food by dangling a fleshy lure in front of its mouth to entice fishes in for a closer look. By then it's too late to escape.

DEEP-SEA ANGLERFISHES

DESCRIPTION AND SIZE Many of the fishes caught in deep-sea trawling nets appear to be fiendish and other-worldly alien creatures. And though they are neither fiendish nor alien, deep-sea anglerfishes are indeed strange animals, especially when we consider their mating habits and the great difference in size between the sexes. Male deep-sea anglerfishes can be one-twentieth the size of the female, with some species less than an inch (2.5 cm) long.

HABITS AND HABITAT Deep-sea anglers live in sunless waters thousands of feet deep. Since finding a mate can be a difficult proposition, the male anglers develop pincer teeth so that when they encounter a female they can hold on tight. Once attached to the female, males become parasites, living through the body of the female. The male's one role is to deliver sperm at the right moment so the process of reproduction can begin.

MYTH The bite of deep-sea anglers is as dangerous as these "sea monsters" are frightening to look at.

TRUTH BEHIND THE MYTH Deep-sea anglerfishes do not attack people. Their peculiar and often frightening appearance is a marvelous result of the evolution of life. Evolution has uniquely adapted such animals to the special conditions where they live.

SPECIAL FEATURES Many deep-sea animals depend on bioluminescence, the production of light by bacteria present in living tissues, to see their way around in the depths of the ocean. In World War II, the Japanese used these bioluminescent bacteria to light their homes during bombing blackouts. Scientists can better understand cell biology and energy transfer through the study of bioluminescence.

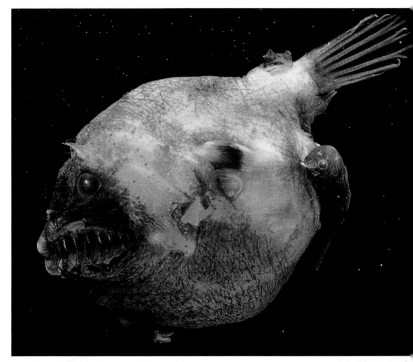

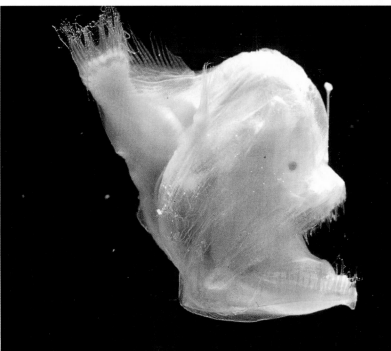

▲ Above: A female anglerfish with male attached.
▲ Below: Behind this image of a creature from another planet is an animal that has adapted to the darkness of the sea by lighting its own way. A bioluminescent organ or lure helps deep-sea anglers find food and mates. If these animals were marveled at for their adaptations to their watery world rather than feared, we wouldn't be in such danger of losing the marvelous diversity of life on Earth.

VENOMOUS AND POISONOUS ANIMALS

DESCRIPTION There is an important distinction between the meanings of "poisonous" and "venomous." Venom is what is physically injected into a victim by spines, stinging cells, and fangs. Poison is a substance which a victim must eat or ingest for there to be an effect. Besides the stingrays already mentioned, there are venomous fishes whose names often give them away: scorpion fish, lionfish, toadfish, stonefish, and stargazers. Like the stingray, these animals have spines, usually running along their back or near their head, which contain venom. Most of these animals live in tropical waters.

HABITS AND HABITAT The venomous fishes mentioned here often lie very still on the ocean floor, or they hover motionless so they won't be observed. Their shape, body fringes, and color help camouflage them.

MYTH Each of these animals injects its venom in a deliberate, unprovoked, and aggressive way.

TRUTH BEHIND THE MYTH Venomous fishes use venom as part of their defensive system when someone steps on or attacks them. They rarely attack unless provoked. Venomous fishes do not bite to deliver their venom. Their spines have venom glands.

SPECIAL FEATURES Many of the chemicals in the venom of venomous fishes are used by scientists to develop antivenins and drugs that can be useful in human medicine. The tetrodoxin or poison of pufferfish, for example, has been studied for its use as an anesthetic in human medicine. Investigations of the venom of cone snails is helping scientists understand how cells communicate information to other cells.

◄ The lionfish (above) and stonefish (below) are two of the undersea world's most familiar venomous fishes. Although both animals can inject a painful venom through spines along their backs and on their fins, the stonefish is recognized as one of the most dangerous of underwater fishes. Once stung, an injection of a powerful antivenin may be the only way for a person to survive.

GLOSSARY

Age of reptiles (REP-tiles)—the period in evolutionary history called the Mesozoic Era, between 225 million and 65 million years ago, when reptiles were the most abundant class of vertebrate, occupying every major habitat, or living area.

alligators (AL-i-GAY-ters)—a group of several species of crocodilians including the American and the Chinese alligator and the caimans. The fourth tooth on an alligator's lower jaw cannot be seen when its jaw is closed.

brackish water—water which contains less salt than the ocean but more salt than is safe to drink; brackish water occurs where a river runs into the ocean, and fresh and salt water mix.

caimans (KAY-muns)—alligatorlike crocodilians that live in Central and South America; examples include the spectacled caiman, with curved ridges of bone connecting their eye sockets, and the black caiman, which grows up to 15 feet (4.6 m) long.

cartilage (KAHR-tuh-lihj)—an elastic tissue that composes most of the skeleton in young vertebrates, but which becomes bone as the animal matures. Sharks and rays are examples of vertebrates whose skeleton remains cartilaginous throughout their lives.

cephalopods (SEF-uh-la-pods)—a group of invertebrates (animals without a backbone) which includes squid, octopuses, and cuttlefish; cephalopods have a distinct head, large eyes, a beak, and tentacles near the mouth.

cornea (KORN-ee-uh)—the outer transparent coating of the eye which covers and protects the eye's pupil and iris.

crocodiles (KROCK-uh-diles)—a group consisting of fourteen species of crocodilians. Among the largest living reptiles, crocodiles live in the tropics of every continent except Europe. The fourth tooth on their lower jaw is visible when the crocodile's mouth is closed.

crocodilians (krock-uh-DILL-ee-ans)—members of an order of reptiles which includes crocodiles, gharials, alligators, and caimans.

crustacean (krus-TAY-shun)—a class of invertebrate animals with a hard outer shell and a jointed body and appendages; lobsters, crabs, shrimp, and barnacles are familiar examples.

denticles (DENT-ik-els)—small teeth or toothlike projections.

docile (DOSS-ul)—harmless to other animals, including humans, because of its passive or unaggressive response to an intruder.

electric fields—all living creatures send out electric pulses produced by their nervous system; animals such as sharks have a special ability to detect these natural electric charges.

gharial (GAR-ee-al)—a kind of crocodilian with a long, extremely narrow, and rounded snout. Its jaws contain more teeth—four rows of twenty-five to thirty interlocking teeth—than any other crocodilian. It lives in the rivers of Pakistan, India, and Upper Burma.

ichthyologist (IK-thee-ahl-uh-gist)—a scientist who studies the biology of fishes.

invertebrates (in-VERT-uh-brates)—animals without a spinal cord or backbone. Familiar invertebrates include insects, sponges, lobsters, and sea stars.

lateral line—(LAT-er-ul)—a system of tiny holes (pores) leading to jelly-filled canals that run along both sides of a fish's body and enable the fish to detect movement in the water.

Loch Ness monster (LOHK NIS)—the name of an unidentified reptilelike animal of which numerous sightings have been recorded in north-central Scotland's Loch (lake) Ness, beginning as far back as the year 565 A.D.

Mikele mbembe (mick-KAY-lee em-BEM-bee)—a legendary creature reported to live in the Congo region of Central Africa, supposedly a dinosaur of sorts.

mollusk (MOHL-usk)—a soft-bodied invertebrate covered by a thick membrane, or mantle.

Mollusks such as clams, mussels, and scallops produce a hard shell made of calcium; octopuses and squid are shell-less.

plankton (PLANK-tun)—tiny animals and plants that live both in fresh and salt water and drift freely with the currents.

poisonous (POISE-on-us)—a plant or animal is said to be poisonous if it causes harm when it is ingested or eaten.

scavenger (SKAV-in-ger)—an animal that feeds on dead organisms.

territory (TER-uh-tor-ee)—an area which animals defend against intruders, especially intruders of their own species; the area can be a few millimeters of space between two barnacles, for example, or several square miles, such as the territory of a herd of buffalo.

venomous (VEN-a-mus)—a plant or animal is said to be venomous if it injects something that causes harm, using a spine, a fang, or a stinging cell, for example.

BIBLIOGRAPHY

SHARKS

Banister, Keith, and Andrew Campbell. *The Encyclopedia of Aquatic Life*. New York: Facts on File, 1985.

Burgess, Robert F. *The Sharks*. New York: Doubleday, 1970.

Castro, Jose I. *The Sharks of North American Waters*. College Sta.: Texas A&M University Press, 1983.

Clark, Eugenie. "Sharks: Magnificent and Misunderstood." *National Geographic*, August 1981.

Grissim, John. "The Perfect Predator." *San Francisco Focus*, August 1990.

Gruber, Samuel, et al. *Ocean Realm*.

Grzimek's Animal Life Encyclopedia. Vol. 4. New York: Van Nostrand Reinhold, 1972.

Milne, Lorus, and Margery Milne. *Invertebrates of North America*. New York: Doubleday, 1972.

Reader's Digest. *Sharks, Silent Hunters of the Deep*. Sydney, London, New York: Reader's Digest Services, 1986.

Springer, Victor G. and Joy P. Gold. *Sharks in Question: The Smithsonian Answer Book*. Washington, D.C.: Smithsonian Institution Press, 1989.

Stafford-Dietsch, Jeremy. *Sharks: A Photographer's Story*. San Francisco: Sierra Club Books, 1987.

PIRANHAS

Axelrod, Herbert. *Breeding Aquarium Fishes: A Complete Introduction*. Neptune City, N.J.: TFH Publications, 1987.

Breland, Osmond P. *Animal Facts and Fallacies*. New York: Harper & Bros., 1948.

Caras, Roger A. *Dangerous to Man*. New York: Holt, Rinehart and Winston, 1964.

Ricciuti, Edward R. *Killers of the Seas*. New York: Walker, 1973.

OCTOPUSES

Caras, Roger. *Dangerous to Man*. New York: Holt, Rinehart & Winston, 1964.

Halstead, Bruce W. *Dangerous Marine Animals*. Ithaca, N.Y.: Cornell Maritime Press, 1980.

Helm, Thomas. *Dangerous Sea Creatures*. New York: Funk & Wagnalls, 1976.

Land, Frank W. *Kingdom of the Octopus*. London: Jarrolds Publishers, 1957.

Ricciuti, Edward. *Killers of the Seas*. New York: Walker, 1973.

KILLER WHALES

Baker, Mary L. *Whales, Dolphins, and Porpoises of the World*. New York: Doubleday, 1987.

Bonner, Nigel. *Whales of the World*. New York: Facts on File, 1989.

Dietz, Tim. *Whales & Man*. Dublin, N.H.: Yankee Books, 1987.

Evans, Peter G. H. *The Natural History of Whales and Dolphins*. New York: Facts on File, 1987.

Harrison, Sir Richard. *Whales, Dolphins and Porpoises*. New York: Facts on File, 1988.

ALLIGATORS AND CROCODILES

Chester, Michael. *Water Monsters*. New York: Grosset & Dunlap, 1973.

Crocodiles and Alligators. New York: Facts on File, 1989.

Graham, Ada, and Frank Graham. *An Audubon Reader—Alligators*. New York: Delacourte Press, 1979.

Halliday, Dr. Tim R. and Dr. Kraig Adler. *The Encyclopedia of Reptiles and Amphibians*. New York: Facts on File, 1986.

Zappalorti, Robert T. *The Amateur Zoologist's Guide to Turtles and Crocodilians*. New York: Stackpole Books, 1976.

GIANT SQUID

F. E. Roper, Clyde and Kenneth Boss. "The Giant Squid." *Scientific American*, April 1982.

I N D E X

Page numbers in *italics* indicate illustrations.

Age of reptiles, 38
Alligators, 35–39
    compared to crocodiles, 36
    skins, hunting of, 38
American alligators. *See* Alligators
Ampullae of Lorenzini, 10, 11
Anesthetics, 52
Anglerfishes, 50, 51
Antivenins, 52
Aquariums, 20, 21, 24
    Steinhart Aquarium, *8, 9*
Architeuthis, 46
Atlantic stingray, 48
Attacks on people, 7, 17, 40, 52
    octopuses, 27
    piranhas, 19–21
    sharks, 14–15
Aurelia aurita, 42

Bacteria light, 51
Barbels, 10
Barracuda, 47
Basking sharks, 13–14
Bioluminescence, 51
Black piranhas, 20
Blue-ringed octopus, 22–23, 27
Body language, *15*, 17
Bottom-feeding sharks, 10
Box jellies (sea wasps), 42
Brackish water, 14
Brain (octopus), 27
Bull shark, 14

Caimans, 37, 39
Camouflage, 52
Cannibal fish. *See* Piranhas
Caribbean reef shark, *15*
Cartilage, 15
Cell biology, 51
Cephalopods, 27
Characidae, 21
Chinese alligator, *36*

Cone snails, 52
Coral polyp, 42
Crocodile Dundee, 37
Crocodiles, 35-39
    compared to alligators, 36
    precautions against, 39
    as predators, 36, 37, 39
    as survivors, 38
Crocodilians, 35-39. *See also*
    Alligators, Crocodiles
Crustaceans, 48
Cyanea capillata, 42

Deep-sea anglerfishes, 51
Denticles, *12,* 13
Dermal denticles. *See* Denticles
Dinosaurs, 38
Diving, *16,* 17, *30-31,* 44
Dragon moray eel, *44-45*

Ears (sharks), 11
Echolocation, *30,* 31
Electromagnetic fields, 10, 11
Endangered species, 33, *34-35,* 36, 38
Energy transfer, 51
Environmental pollution, 33
Eskimos, 33
Eyes, *10*
    of cephalopods, 27
    of giant squid, 46
    of horseshoe crabs, 41
    of octopuses, 27
    of sharks, 10, 15

Finback whale, *33*
Food for humans, 21, 48
    goosefish (monkfish), 50

Gharial, 37
Giant squid, 46
Giant stingray, *49*
Gill arches, *32*
Goosefish, 50
Gray reef shark, *15,* 17
Great white shark, *8, 9,* 14, *16*
    See also Sharks

Habitats, 33, 38
Hogan, Paul, 37

Horn shark, 10
Horseshoe crabs, 41
Hugo, Victor, 23
Hunting, 33, 38

Indo-Pacific crocodile, 37
Indo-Pacific smooth stingray, 48
Ink, 26, 46
    giant squid, 46
    octopus, *26*
Intelligence, 27, 31
International Whaling Commission, 33

Jaws, 13
Jellyfishes, 42, *43*

Killer whales, 29-33
    food consumption of, 32
    as predators, 29, 31-32
    size of, 31
Kraken, *2,* 46

Lateral line system, 10, 11
Lemon sharks, 10
Lionfish, 52
Lion's mane jellyfish, *42-43*
Loch Ness monster, 40
Low-frequency vibrations, 10

Manta ray, 48, *49*
Mariculture, 46
Marine Mammal Protection Act of 1972, *33*
Medicines, 41, 32, 46, 52
Mediterranean moray eel, 44
Megamouth, 14, 40
Monkfish, 50
Moratorium on whaling, 33
Moray eels, 44, *45*
Mythical animals, *2,* 40, 46

Nematocysts, 42
Neon tetras, *20,* 21
Nervous system, 10,
    of giant squid, 46
    octopus, 27
Nile crocodile, 37
Nurse shark, 10

Octopuses, 23-27